Vindication

Post
20th Century
Poems

First Edition

Vindication

Post
20th Century
Poems

DIANNE VAN DER MEER

TATE PUBLISHING
AND ENTERPRISES, LLC

Published by Tate Publishing & Enterprises, LLC
127 E. Trade Center Terrace | Mustang, Oklahoma 73064 USA
1.888.361.9473 | www.tatepublishing.com

Tate Publishing is committed to excellence in the publishing industry. The company reflects the philosophy established by the founders, based on Psalm 68:11,
"The Lord gave the word and great was the company of those who published it."

Published in the United States of America

ISBN: 978-1-63063-393-6
1. Poetry/America/African America
2. Subjects & Themes/General.
13.11.12

DEDICATION

To Mother

Yvonne

Vindication:
Post 20th Century Poems

"I wrote Vindication with a deep level of
consciousness that originated not from my head
but from the wells of my heart."

Dianne Van der Meer

TABLE OF CONTENTS

INTRODUCTION

indication: Post 20th Century Poems insightfully recounts, through my lens, everyday living, political blunders, religious outrage, economic woes and social faux pas that have plagued the early 21st Century.

I expressed, without walls, the freedom of my global surroundings that is reflective of these poems; having lived in the Caribbean, England and the United States of America.

Storytelling has always been a part of my culture in Trinidad and Tobago. One way in which it manifests itself in the literary public square, is through "Calypso." These well thought out, well composed poetic songs often tell a story of social or political satire that is not only entertaining but educational. Calypso expresses the skillfulness of the artist, for example, by using humor, verisimilitude or story-telling in song, lyrics, sonnet and music to get a point across. In writing poetry, I drew from the Calypso art form of my rich, inherited culture. I also incorporated in this body of work, Bible-style poetry. I have been influenced by the greatest poets in Bible poetry: King David in the book of Psalms; King Solomon in the book of Songs of

Solomon; and, John who wrote, under inspiration and instruction, the book of Revelation.

Each stanza of my poems documents facts or an expression of my perception. My primary goal in *Vindication* is to recapture, through poetry, a glimpse of life in the Post 20th Century and raise questions, for example, are we really advancing as a society, when women are still being abused at alarming rates and young boys forcibly sodomized by spiritual leaders, that vowed to protect, or, where human trafficking is a growing phenomenon? Has the Post 20th century era taken a step backwards into barbarism as knowledge increases? Is man getting wickeder and wiser? You decide.

In this book, I attempted to blend a cross-cultural flavor in my poems with an accent on Afro-Caribbean English style influences. This makes *Vindication* a different and more interesting read. I topically organized the poems for easy flow of reading. Covering a wide range of issues and interchangeably using American and English style poetry, I wrote poems about love, pride, health, religion, politics, zionism, abuse, animals, insects, nature, places and things; in ways that will educate, inform, encourage, entertain, strengthen and raise the consciousness of the reader.

In this delivery form, I experienced challenges zipping in and out of American and English styles of poetry, although I embrace a meshing of both styles. For example, when I transition from the use of Caribbean dialect and pun, to the use of American imagery within its social culture; my pen wants to make the shift but my writing flow is still drawing from a Caribbean English influence. It is the same problem that I sometimes encounter when switching from, for example, spelling "Check" (in the American grammatical form) to spelling "Cheque" (in the Caribbean and British grammatical forms).

I applaud Caribbean born Poet Laureate Derek Walcott for having made this transition with great ease. American style poetry is more contemporary and unconventional with an imagery of self and improvisation; while, English style poetry tends to be more formal and conventional with greater emphasis on tone and place.

In *Vindication*, I deliberately chose, as a personal preference, to use upper case letters at the beginning of each line. I used punctuation marks in some of the poems; and in others, no punctuation marks were used, as a matter of stylistic freedom that perhaps is more reflective of my global and cultural-historical socialization.

In some ways my attempts at American style poetry was influenced by the American poet Robert Frost, in his delivery of rhymed lyrics and his expression of joy and trials of life. And, undoubtedly I am influenced by Harlem Renaissance women writers, with whom I share an uncanny connection and great admiration. For example, over 100 years ago, Jessie Redmon-Fauset, wrote about the oppression of women. Fauset identifies, in her writings, the social plight of women, their suffering and the sacrifices they had to make on their journey, in pursuit of happiness. In writing *Vindication*, Fauset's 1929 novel "Plum Bun" raised my sense of consciousness to write on similar issues that are still affecting women, 100 years later.

I can identify with Fauset's writings having myself experienced abuse, sexism, racism, being economically marginalized and raised children as a single parent, but I kept on moving. To borrow a phrase from 20th Century Poet Laureate Maya Angelo, "Still I Rise." In writing *Vindication*, I drew strength from other Harlem Renaissance pillars like Zora Neale Hurston, Juanita Harrison and Elizabeth Laura Adams to mention a few.

Adams found refuge in poetry, classical music and religion. I have found my refuge in poetry, dance, classical music, sharing a personal relationship with my Lord and Saviour Jesus Christ and a daily prayer regiment. Adams was interested in raising consciousness by sounding an alarm, through her writings, on racism in the church. *Vindication: Post 20th Century Poems* speaks to abuse, sexism, disorderly conduct and the misappropriation of vested power within the church. Adam's expressions, it is speculated, rendered her silent in the anthologies and history books. A price she paid for opening the door as a trail blazer and breaking the silence. Once opened and exposed that door could never be the same again. It was left ajar giving *Vindication: Post 20thCentury Poems* an entry point to revisit. Hopefully, *Vindication: Post 20th Century Poems* would not be silent in the anthologies of history.

Harlem Renaissance woman poet Juanita Harrison inspired and amazed me as I wrote *Vindication: Post 20th Century Poems*. Harrison was formally uneducated. She worked as a maid and traveled extensively with her employer in the course of her employment. Harrison tapped into her non-formal global education and used it to her advantage. What amazed me about this sister was that, in spite of her limitations and in a period of economic depression, she realized her dream as a Poet. In writing *Vindication: Post 20th Century Poems*, I am realizing my dream as a poet, while facing much personal trauma. Perhaps it is this very one factor of personal trauma that liberated me to fish in the depth of my soul to frame poetry.

I give thanks for the strength and consolation that I have gleaned from those that have gone before me, for example, Harlem Renaissance poet and writer Zora Neale Hurston. She was a Howard University educated black woman who perhaps, disappointed by the lack of progress and respect for the social struggle and her work as a renaissance artist, returned to Florida where she grew up. She found employment there as a maid and died poor in a welfare home. I empathize with her frustration but in *Vindication: Post 20th Century Poems* I embrace her spirit. Zora Neale Hurston is said to have approached life as, "a series of encounters and challenges," much to her credit, accomplishments and achievements.

I drew perseverance and hope from Emily Dickinson, a great American poet. Dickinson's work was never published in her lifetime but she kept on writing and disseminating her poems, sending them to a publisher and as gifts to friends and family. Dickinson was clearly demonstrating confidence in herself and her work. Emily Dickinson refused to allow the demon of rejection and the ignorance of others to break her spirit. That is my stance as I share *Vindication.*

Vindication's motif was in some ways also inspired by the blunt and graphic account that twentieth-century poet Robert Pinsky brought to his work, as he captured the Triangle Shirt Factory Fire of 1911 in his poem "Shirts." The fire claimed 146 lives and Pinsky through the poem brought attention to Labor oppression and advocated for better working conditions. *Vindication: Post 20th Century Poems* also highlights social situations and voices the need for social change. For example, the poem, "Pack Fever" describes an alleged Juno Game effect in which, it was alleged that, teenage high school students planned to raise their kids together by getting pregnant in a pack, while still in high school.

Vindication: Post 20th Century Poems is for individuals, book clubs and primarily students. Academic institutions will find it useful for the purpose of dissecting and discussing social issues as well as poetic forms. Instructors may elicit students' thoughts and feelings about the poems and thus bring alive the past as a memorable way of connecting to history. Others may wish to reflect on the content as a prelude to social and political action. This book is completed but the work is unfinished because the twenty-first century is still unfolding.

PART 1:

INSECTS AND ANIMALS

Mosquito

By Dianne Van der Meer

A mosquito is a ruthless
Ridiculous little creature
Sounding its invisible wings
Like a stampede of wild horses
Violently racing

With a pathetic name like mosquito,
Who wants to be bothered
By this little insignificant creature
Announcing itself in my area

Flying around in the dark, buzzing in foolish stupor
Long thin legs
Eyes there but not there
Bodies smaller than a centimeter
Some with white stripes like a zebra

Dancing in the air
As if celebrating
Before attacking
Injecting, now female sucking

Bites feeling deadly
Burning, itching, so disgusting

At last! I caught one
Killing it, dead
Proof that this blood sucker
Raped my leg

A speck of blood filling my hand
This mosquito crushed
In the palms of my hands

Looks like two pints of blood
T'is speck in my hand
This blood thirsty little creature
In the class of a vampire
Needing my blood, reproduction

Now my soft delicate skin
Bright red
Oozing with inflammation
Looking like strawberries
Non edible, oh so painful

My skin screaming
In protest of this violation
I vote for mosquito extinction
Kill them all
Wishful thought

My skin itching
My nails scratching
Spreading the infection
Itching all over
A mosquito is the worse insect ever.

Groundhog

By Dianne Van der Meer

Groundhog Day comes again,
Fondly remembering February Second
It's my daughter's birthday,
It's Super bowl Sunday.

A day for the Groundhog
To run and play
Getting out of the way
Making way for winter to go away
On this Cloudy day
Leaving its burrow to run away

Hibernating all winter
Appearing February Second
Tradition say
A sunny day
Groundhog can't run and play
Returning to its burrow
In the thick of day

A superstitious sign
Winter delay
That's what the farmers say

Appearing from underground
In the dead of winter
Tantalizing media interest all over
Groundhog making evening news
A sunny day, winter stay

Groundhog's shadow did or did not appear,
Television coverage
It's a ritual every year
Groundhog is king
Creating excitement in the atmosphere

An official day declared
Every February second, Groundhog Day
In the United States of America
Creating excitement in the atmosphere

Well dressed men
In black scissors tail suits
And tall black hats
Waiting for the groundhog to appear
To forecast winter predictions
For the newscasters to hear
Marking the occasion, this superstition.

Birds

By Dianne Van der Meer

Shooting up and down
Aimlessly in the sky
Soaring higher than the highest building
As if can't die

Dipping to the ground for convenience
Food
Non-permanence

Soaring back into the sky
Where freedom presides

Flying in a row,
In military style,
Shooting off the roof
As if bungee jumping
Without a parachute.

Bowel Movements

By Dianne Van der Meer

Moving the Bowels,
A spontaneous event,
All life must excrete,
The urge to go, everyone gets.
Bowel movements
The great equalizer
Can't escape it, just like death
The urge to go, everyone gets

Can't explain it
Some have trouble doing it
Going is necessary for good health
Bowel Movements
No respecter of age, race, or socio-economic health,
It feels great! After this spontaneous event.

PART 2:

FORECLOSURE

Templar

By Dianne Van der Meer

The Pope of France
Grew up with Philip the IV
This Pope was placed
For Philip's agenda and support,
Never leaving France for Rome was this Pope
Making it less effective for helping the crusaders, in Rome

Pope and Philip dying in the same year
Same year Knights' Templar Grand Master, Jacques DeMolay
Pronounced a curse, to their despair
Making room for Rome
With Christian Crusaders there

The Medieval Knights Templar
Rising to power
The year 1129, the church gave them all power,
Granting them usual favor

Exploiting their authority,
Abusing their power,
Expanding their base,
In hieratical secret order
Offering high profile loans
Slashing gold
Roslyn Castle, who knows?

Created they, the banking system
Created they, loans and credit systems
Created they, this money exchange system
Power galore

Lording it over the ones they once nurtured and adored
Templar planted a seed,
For the modern day killer, foreclosure

Foreclosure this modern day killer
Banks moving like Knights Templar
Secret order

With attractive loan programs to remember,
They offer
Vowing to help the community to recover,

True, we believe
Proud, we are
Owning a house for the first time,
Feeling like a Czar

No down payment,
Adjustable Mortgage,
Didn't even understand
What we were signing

True, she believed
Signing away,
True, she believed
Trusting the Templar
To this day

Now cost of living gone up
Mortgages doubling up,
This she could not see
Saying, "The bank did not tell me.
Did the Knights Templar trick me?

"Now, off my house must go,
Back to a new mortgage company
I don't even know.
Lost my investment, I did.
To those sharks that took it, without a blink."

Now homeless, she can see
But no more money
No more strength to fight the enemy
Seems like the Templar has surfaced again
In the Twenty-First Century
History repeating itself.

Yo Yo

By Dianne Van der Meer

Yo Yo's
Warning of the danger
In a dream
Of the three wolves

Yes, said she
I saw the wolves
Charging they came
Into the church
Not sent for me
'Tis for you Pastor, all three

Hear them,

Like vicious dogs roaring,
Hoping to silence you, Pastor
In the church
Wolf one, wolf two, wolf three
It felt so real

Conquered them in the dream, I did

Awake

Failed in my battle with cancer bring
It is not the Cancer
That's killing me
Nor the wolves numbers one, two and three

It's the stress I felt and held this year,
The pain of Foreclosure, the wear and tear,
Now, I must sleep,
It's time to end
Foreclosure is behind me
I have trusted God to the end.

Yo Yo sleeps.

Foreclosure

By Dianne Van der Meer

Foreclosure, the four-letter bad word
Spelled with more than four letters
Foreclosure, a twenty-first century killer

Families collapsing
Banks going under
It's that kind of pressure

Foreclosure, big investments
Corporations under fire
Exposing their dirty laundry
Thanks to foreclosure

Foreclosure that four-letter word
Growing stronger and stronger

People running from their houses
People being pushed from their houses
Not quite understanding
But only feeling
The vicious effects of foreclosure

Blamed for suicides and bankruptcy too
Blamed for belly-up businesses
This evil foreclosure do
Coming unexpectedly
For the majority and the few.

Bernanke

By Dianne Van der Meer

Stock market haggling,
Dipping and crashing,
Economic systems revolving
Only market crash of 1929 comparing

Diversion, debates over whether it's
A recession or depression
That's not the real question

Budget cuts daily
Affecting social service programs
Unemployment, no recovery,
The cry
All over the country

Another hit in the cost of living index we see,
Bernanke announcing interest rates going up again
Yet failing to admit to reality
We are in a greater economic crisis,
Than our neighbors overseas.

Gypsum

By Dianne Van der Meer

Chinese Drywall* manufacturers
Fulfilling supply on demand
From American distributors
For building materials
To home owners

Undermining America's
Manufacturers with cheaper prices
Consumers saving dollars
But getting poorer
Suppliers' profit margins rising higher

Gypsum

Two boards packed like a sandwich
Sulfur toxin properties
Hazardous waste between it
Drywalls slipping into America
Satisfying demand for
Construction throughout the region

Gypsum

---

* Drywall: A wall that is constructed with prefabricated material, a plasterboard

Silent killer
Toxic fumes
The perpetrator
Fly Ash neatly tucked away
As the main property in drywall
The sandwich for which
We must now pay

Gypsum

Defective drywalls
Seeping toxin all over

Gypsum

Allowing, not learning
From the toxic pet food
And tainted cough syrup
Previously imported
From China and others

Gypsum

Insurance companies
Pulling the plug on homeowners' insurability
Scared of the drywall frenzy

While drywalls' slowly killing
Mortgage bills still must be paying
Creating more foreclosures; paining
No one seems to have the answer; only blaming

With no bail-out plan in sight
Rumbling in the industry; big fight
Regulators locked in bureaucracy
Homeowners now paying the penalty.

PART 3:

NANTUCKET

Nantucket, the Beautiful

By Dianne Van der Meer

Nantucket, the Beautiful,
Oh so serene,
The best time to vacation there,
Is the end of September, I swear.

When the weather is cool,
The winds so soft,
Beaming sunlight, changing leaves,
Gentle breeze,
Signifying a new Fall season.

Big sales, signs in store windows,
Bargains galore,
Marking the end of the season,
No more to outpour.

Visitors gone till another season,
Back to the quiet of life
For this reason
Nantucket, oh the beautiful,
How your light continues to shine,
See you next season.

Tick Tact

By Dianne Van der Meer

Nantucket, a place to remember,
But don't get bitten by a tick.
Not pleasant to remember.
Medical problems flare up,
Months later,
I do remember,
Gee Whiz, it was that tick that bit, from Nantucket.

Utility Waste

By Dianne Van der Meer

Garbage disposal day in Nantucket
A cultural experience
Driving along the streets,
No garbage to be seen,
Oh! What an experience
On garbage disposal day, in Nantucket

Pick up the garbage around the back, they say
Utility waste workers
Know the way
To our back yards,
To fetch the garbage
On garbage day

No garbage displaying
On the side walks
On garbage days
They say:
We must keep our image in Nantucket; everyday.

The Rotary

By Dianne Van der Meer

No, not the Rotary Club
But an intersection
In Nantucket

Where the rotary is
Called a traffic circle
Where the roundabout is
Called a traffic circle

Nantucket library building
The Atheneum
See that large "H" letter
At Prospect Street?

Pointing to the Hospital,
Looking edible
Like the "H" is borrowed,
From a can of Campbell's Vegetable Soup
Pointing the way
Approaching traffic circle, that way.

Light House

By Dianne Van der Meer

Nantucket Light House is shifting,
Getting weaker from its roots,
Sea water claiming

Geologists still trying to figure out,
Why nature's reclaiming
Why land's shifting
From under the light house

Nantucket light house falling,
Rooted up by sea water shifting,
Moved back to safety,
Now moving it again?
That's crazy!
Light house, shifting, shifting, shifting

Looks like the light house talking,
Depicting signs of what's coming,
Change in bio-diversity coming,
Change in cultural diversity coming,
Change in demographic composition coming,
Change, Change
Nantucket's light house talking change.

Canopache[*]

By Dianne Van der Meer

Where the sky seems bluer
The cloud softly and sporadically
Shadowing the blue

Grouped like cotton in a pack
On a supermarket shelf
Yet not as dead

The clouds come alive in splendor
It's a perfect ten weather day
On this island of Nantucket,
A day to remember

Streaking across the sky,
A cloud extending in a straight line
Going around as to measure the
Circumference of the sky
See the birds fly

Leaves passively moving
In the light breeze
A place of peace
It's the first day of Fall
Bright sun, a cool breeze

---

[*]   Canopache: A place of peace

Soon the green is gone
Trees shedding leaves
See the foliage in colorful splendor
Then comes Old Man Winter,
If you please.

Culture Shock

By Dianne Van der Meer

Sunflowers still blooming
As if to say good morning

Cars whisking by
Free of stop lights,
No traffic Jam in sight.

Where is the McDonalds, I say
Sorry, none.

A place without any fast food chains, pray
No traffic lights either, getting in the way

Where the buses stop running
All winter long, everyday
No trains either, running through town
It's the price we pay
To preserve Nantucket this way.

Siasconset, the Pretty

By Dianne Van der Meer

Journeying through the city of Siasconset*
Where the streets are painted
And the
Sun looks forever set,

Eighteenth Century cottages,
In all sizes and beauty

Telling a story
Of old Siasconset
In its hey-day glory

A glimpse of the past
Preserving the future
A glimpse of the past
Siasconset, still standing
In great splendor

A glimpse of the past
Preserving the future
Pioneers now gone
Siasconset still standing
In great splendor

---

* Siasconset: A town on the Island of Nantucket in Massachusetts

Ancestors long gone
Their spirits a reminder
Of the Native American storytellers
Siasconset once their home
Nantucket their land long ago
Presence felt

Life remains humble in Siasconset
Still have to travel to town to market

But not so humble
When you look around
Each cottage house bearing its own name
Some with the year built in glory and fame.

The Main Street Rotary
A meeting point for historic tours

In front of the bike rack
Starts the story of biodiversity,
Nantucket's history
And much more
Siasconset, the pretty.

Frozen Flower

By Dianne Van der Meer

Nantucket, buy
Hand crafted jewelry from locals,
Depicting island flowers,
Highly priced,
Tantalizing, frozen beauty
An unreachable power

Nantucket,
I hate to leave thee,
You inspire me,
With your sumptuous beauty.

Columbus

By Dianne Van der Meer

Columbus, oh Columbus,
How I long for thee,
To warm me
On this bleak fall day
In Nantucket, I be

The sky is grey
As the houses be
Columbus, oh Columbus
It's such a gloomy day,
Cold, without thee

I left you at home
But the cold came early
Columbus, oh Columbus,
How I miss thee

I brought a lighter coat to wear.
Now how I wish you were here
Columbus, oh Columbus,
My warm winter coat,
How I long for thee.

PART 4:

TELEVISION

The View

By Dianne Van der Meer

Walters' brain child
A mid-morning talk show,
Women talking for so,

Who would ever think
Mid-morning ratings could soar so?
Every politician wants to be on the show
'Cause them women, talk for so.

A mid-morning talk show,
Now so mainstream, you know,
'Cause them women, talk for so.

Chatter, chatter, talking over each other,
Like a fish market scene
From a third world country, they gather
Everyone's voice wants to be heard over the other

Voices all at the same time,
As if competing with each other
I tell you so.
Them women, talk for so,

Drilling their guest
Like well diggers,
Drawing out the answers
With bait like master fishers
Sometimes never agreeing with each other
The View, changing talk show format, forever.

PART 5:

COURT

Family Court

By Dianne Van der Meer

Arriving at the court house, a challenge
Finding the court room, a feeling of imbalance
Bodies, warming benches in the hallway

Lawyers, talking to clients
Clients, talking to lawyers
Facial expressions telling the story,
Tension feeling like disarray

Inside, family matters,
Judge hearing petitions
One after the other,
Fast moving like a production line,
Involving kids, separation agreements,
Restraining orders,
Much deeper

A different culture,
The smell of anger in the air
This one man sitting, waiting
Face bowed in hands,
Eyes closed as if sleeping
Projecting innocence, as a victim at hand

Perpetrator playing victim,
Hands covering face,
Revealing himself, an angry man
Vexed at being caught and exposed,
Looking for sympathy,
Another form of control,
Revealing his true identity

The real victim
On the opposite side,
Sitting, waiting,
Silently observing this passer by.

Guilty but Free

By Dianne Van der Meer

All Rise! Court in session
Caught in the Act
He whispers to another
I've been in Jail for four days
Before posting bail
Today I am taking a guilty plea
If they go set me free
I know jail already

Case Called

Do you understand your guilty plea, Sir?
Beckons the Judge from the bench
Yes, Your Honor
The Judge explaining the plea bargain
The man understanding
Free, Free, Guilty but Free.

Restraining Order

By Dianne Van der Meer

Restraining order, a legal piece of paper
Bearing weight, if the perpetrator surrenders,
To the terms of the paper

Bearing no weight
To a mind of disorder
Who ignores,
Terms of the paper,
In-spite-of penalties for breaking the order

Restraining Order
A wise protector
But does not guarantee deliverance
Protect yourself, beyond the paper.

Default

By Dianne Van der Meer

No, Your Honor, my client is not here,

When last was he here?
Did he ever appear?

A few weeks ago, Your Honor
When I told him he must be here
Have not heard from him since, Your Honor
How could he dare not be here?

Default, shouting from the bench,
Issuing a warrant for his arrest

Next!

Time to Pay

By Dianne Van der Meer

Packed like sardines in a can
This court room

Filled, of young men

Faces telling a story
Of shock and humility
Everyone denying, saying
It was not me

Treating me, *guilty*
Until proven innocent
But it was not me
A case of mistaken identity
All telling the same story
A case of mistaken identity

I am here
To say, it was not me
See the judge looking at me?
Sir, a case of mistaken identity
All telling the same story

My court appointed lawyer
Treating me like I am a statistic

Help!

Now in trouble
Remembering my mother's warning
Boy, keep out of trouble
For you just a number to them people

The lawyer asking how much I can pay
For the judge will ask her this day

I told her none to pay
I ain't working no-way
Well, we must tell the judge something this day
How about asking for time to pay?
That's okay.

Beep Beep

By Dianne Van der Meer

A young man sitting on the courthouse step
Waiting for the doors to open
A woman said,
Get up, son this is court
So what! I am tired, said he

In court you must play the part
You must dress the part, said she
To that he does agree.

Doors Open
No cell phones please, guard shouting
Beep Beep, scanner sounding,

Step aside, Sir
Beckons the guard
No, No, I good to go, said he

Step aside, Sir
I'm clean man, said he
Just lift your arms
We must check everybody

Now, you good to go
I tell you, ah clean man, said he
I am only doing my job, you know
Both men's eyes viciously connecting.

Dress the Part

By Dianne Van der Meer

Inside a packed court room
Only lawyers dressed in suit and tie
Pearls and fancy dark color suits, the style

Young men,
T-shirts hanging over,
Baggy pants seem to be the order,
Except for this one black fella[*]

With red shirt hanging out of his pants,
Wearing collar and tie,
Staring into the ceiling,
Standing in style

Whispering to him, a stranger I am
Son, let me be your mother today.
Put your shirt in your pants all the way.

Watching as if wanting to say,
Who are you lady?
Get out of my way!
Put your shirt in your pants all the way,
I quickly say.

---

[*] Fella: A boy or man

In obedience but shocked,
Exiting the door
Returning shortly after,
Saying, thanks mama and more
That's my case calling now.

Standing in front of the judge,
Shirt in pants all the way,
Hopefully, his appearance made a difference on this day.

Piercing Stare

By Dianne Van der Meer

Must tell my story
Not knowing which one will defend me
Oh, it's me, it's me, cried he
I'm the one chosen to tell your story
The Prosecutor

Young and bold
Just out of law school
No experience
A clever old soul
He will tell my story

Fresh out of law school
Vigorous is he
Yes, he is the one to defend me

Enthusiastic at that
With a dead man stare
Open eye lids, alert
Spread like a fan
Not even a wink
Just a piercing stare

Tell me your story, dear
Good grounds,
But I cannot build my case,
Unless you tell me;
What happened next, my dear?

So fresh it was to relive
Telling the ordeal in tears
Feeling alone
Didn't want to go home

I will defend you to my best
Let the court do the rest

When the State makes its case clear
You just have to wait and see how you fare
Just tell the truth and trust God, my dear
It's all you can do
Court is not always fair
So get a good night's sleep and be prepared.

PART 6:

IMMIGRATION

Green Card

By Dianne Van der Meer

Fifteen years waiting for her Green Card
Green card not even green in color
But it bears power to remember
Making her a bona fide resident,
In a super power
United States of America

Fifteen years waiting for her Green Card
Accusing her Pastor of blocking it
After the Church applied for it
Woman lamenting
After working hard to
Earn it
But how could this be?
I refuse his inappropriate advances, said she

Woman lamenting, when Pastor had the power
He silently hid my approval letter
It was
Two years later
I saw the letter
He had no answer

Transgression it will be, said she
To lay in fornication and adultery
With Pastor, a married man

Woman lamenting, not me!
Thank God, I still have my dignity
Without my green card, I am still somebody.

PART 7:

RELIGION

How Awesome

By Dianne Van der Meer

How awesome are you, Lord
How awesome, are you
When the prophet hid in the cave,
Not even Jezebel knew.

But the raven passed by
With food from you
How awesome are you, Lord
How awesome, are you

When the children of Israel
Saw only sea ahead,
The sound of Pharaoh's Chariots
Behind,
Sounding, like missiles overhead

The Red Sea miraculously parted
Letting them through,
A sign from you
How awesome are you, Lord
How awesome, are you

You fed the winged woman
In the wilderness,
Her place of safety,
She flew
How awesome, are you
Then that angry serpent,
Revengeful at your creation,
Sent,
A fury of flood waters
In that dry secret place,
To ravish your daughter

Commanding the parched earth
To drink on this day,
Drunken by the flood waters,
The earth that day
The woman safely out of the way
How awesome are you, Lord
How awesome are you.

But God

By Dianne Van der Meer

Waking up in the twilight
Still in the land of the living
Hear the birds chirping
Through my gloomy eyes

T'is winter in the dark of twilight
No birds in sight
I heard them chirping
Through my gloomy eyes
'Cause I woke up alive

Only in God's hands, my revelation and safety lies
Only in God's hands could this not be a lie
With the enemy so close by
Feeling my watery eyes, pain
No place to hide

The invisibility of God's presence captured
My sagging eyes
But God
Had it not been for her presence on my side

What God has done for me, she'll do for you
Knowing "But God," you'll make it too.

Righteousness

By Dianne Van der Meer

Righteousness you cannot buy
Righteousness you cannot sell
Righteousness like Salvation
Free, and others can tell

Righteousness is not about the clothes you wear
Righteousness is not about the gifts you display
Righteousness is about the character of man,
Shown all the way.

Now Gone

By Dianne Van der Meer

Both now gone
Void left deep
Wishing their return
Fountain seek

Tossing coins
Wishing
Echoing deep
Shadow see
Watching back at me
A reflection of self

Me in them, them in me
Cherished memories
The cycle be.

Queen Esther

By Dianne Van der Meer

Purim, commanded the Lord,
Always remember
A day of deliverance,
From the hands of the slaughter,
A celebration forever,
Thanks! Queen Esther.

Roll Call

By Dianne Van der Meer

Eat the Roll
What's the Roll?
The Roll's the Scroll
Eat the Roll
Why the Roll?
To receive Revelation of the Scroll

Prophet John in Revelation 3:10
Was instructed to eat the Roll
Prophet Ezekiel in Ezekiel 3:8
Was instructed to eat the Roll
Good for the Prophets
We must understand it
Working in our lives; the prophetic

Eat the Roll
Must digest it, to ignite it
Receiving revelation knowledge
At its highest

What's the ingredient in it?
The Breath of Life,
Longevity, wrap in it,
Can't escape it,
Must, share it.

Bashan

By Dianne Van der Meer

Like cows of Bashan* they frolic, grazing in the sun
Like the cedars of Lebanon
Waiting for the second coming of the son
Standing, unmovable and ruthless
Some wearing gowns
Speaking from vipers in their tongues

Weekly they gather, calling it church
Exhibiting poor character, the son hurts.
Through a religious spirit, church folks manifesting dirt
While counting down the son's last days on earth
Waiting for the second coming of the son, wasting time
Evil hearts cannot reign with the Christ
Left to burn in the sun
Missing the true revelation.

---

* Bashan: A wide fertile place

Zondoly

By Dianne Van der Meer

Living in the firmament
Stretching from sky to ground,
Riding the ladder
Stretching from beyond

Living in the firmament
Stretching from sky to ground
Riding the ladder
Stretching from beyond

Touching beneath the waters,
Stretching from sky to ground
Making a destructive sound
Zondoly, was cast down.
With fallen angels in tow
Ready for a show

Zondoly, the best musician in town,
Was cast down,
From heaven's hemisphere,
To earth below,
For wanting to be, top dog in heaven's show

Disguised with enchantments
Marvelous light, but dark
Zondoly, luring man,
Big problems
Battle of evil and good, wrong and right,
Deus ex machina* intercedes.

Zondoly winning, victims seeing not seeing
Hearing not hearing
Zondoly winning, victims alive
Living in the congregation of the dead
While still alive.

---

* Deus ex Machina: intervention of a god to solve a seemingly insoluble problem

Zion

By Dianne Van der Meer

Zion, calling out to the assembly of nations
Remembering the Holy City significance
Zion, speaking out to the Assembly of Nations
Saying, "not your business,"
It's a holy war, that was set in motion

A spiritual war these two nations

Brother versus Brother
Blessed is one brother, this rich nation
Covenant promise, belonging to the other
Fighting for water
Water flowing, new Cisterns to discover
Blood shedding, claiming the cisterns under.

Dear God

By Dianne Van der Meer

Thank you for this day.
Please help me to see my way.
I lift my prayers to you today.
With lifted hands
I am going all the way.

Free me from sin.
Cleanse me from unrighteousness.
Clear my way.
Protect me this day.
For this is my only prayer today.

Mother Theresa

By Dianne Van der Meer

Mother Teresa, went into labor
When she saw, the state of India
Mother Theresa, forming a new order
To labor for India

Wrapping herself in sheets
Giving from beyond her needs
Birthing many sons and daughters
Without penetration or artificial insemination

Possessed by labor for the nation
This special woman.

Waltz

By Dianne Van der Meer

Looking at Joy
Wedding bells ring
The meshing of two cultures bring

Traveling thousands of miles away
Oh, so happy
A thousand miles, seeming like one mile, each way
Cheerful

When that glorious day came
Excitement filling the air
With pomp, frolic and fanfare,
There was no despair
Only sixteenth-century chapel music, filling the air

Three months later, feeling the bite,
Of a sleeping lion that seemed to ignite.
This could not be true
So dark, was he
Functioning in the light, of that big city

Like drums rolling,
The lion exploding,
I saw the fox escaping,
From within the lion vibrating,

Now beyond the pain,
Fox, in clear sight
Must move on without regret, less regress

Faith, dictates destiny
Destiny calls
Moving blindly forward,
On the promises of God,
Into the unknown, Faith,
Wanting to crumble,
No longer grow,
Faith saying, No!
God will provide
All the way,
He is more than able,
To show you the way.

Lion Sleeps

By Dianne Van der Meer

The Lion, pretending to be a Lamb
With the venom of a serpent
Ready to prey, with vengeance

Manifesting the squeeze of an anaconda,
Stifling
Never knew men of God behaved this way
Leading by godly example, a requirement, God's way
So disappointing, this man of God

Put not your Confidence in man, Solomon, say
The prophet Micah, did say
When sitting in darkness the Lord shall be a light, any day
Please Lord, Light, I pray
As the book of Micah
Inspired me this day

Psalm 119:105
"God's word is a lamp to my feet
And a light to my path,"
God's Promise
Now when I look where my destiny leads
No Lion could stop me
Or block my way
Because the peace of Christ
Rules in my heart today
God's promises, prevails.

Destiny

By Dianne Van der Meer

My soul cries to the Lord.
Do I go forward?
Do I go backward?
Why me?
I am a child of destiny.

Need to fine-tune you
For this hour,
Precious flower

A child of God
Must be tested
The nature of Salvation
Requires it.

Endure

By Dianne Van der Meer

The Lord made good
For the day of good,

The Lord made evil
For the day of evil

The rain falls on the just,
And, on the unjust, too,

So dry your eyes
Life goes on
I am with you, said, the Lord

You will never see another day like this.
It is forever gone.
Tomorrow, you do not want to miss,
It's a new day every dawn

So dry your tears, precious flower
Get back in the race.
The race is not for the swift,
But for those who stay

Great is your struggle,
In it is your reward,
So dry your eyes, precious flower
Your weakness is made perfect in my strength
I'll help you endure.

The Head

By Dianne Van der Meer

It starts at the top.
The whole body is sick,
A revelation of the heart,
A spiritual hit

It starts from the top,
If the head is sick,
A revelation of the heart,
The whole body is sick.
An inside hit.

When leadership is corrupt,
The whole body is sick,
Becoming contaminated,
Heart disease
A spiritual hit

So be careful where you go
Must diligently
Guard your spirit from
Becoming contaminated, you know

Some Charismatic leaders
Truly make you wonder
But guard your spirit
From these imposters

Wisdom and discernment
You must know
Add understanding, with daily prayer,
As your remedy
And do not fear.

God's House

By Dianne Van der Meer

God's house is a place of worship
God's house is a place for the paining
God's house is a house of transformation
Where the hurting and lame can leave their pain

God's house is not for Entertainment
Many will pay at Judgment
For the lives they misled
When they allowed
Entertainment

This one church counting numbers
Their margin line the mighty dollar
Desperation taking over
Entertainment their
Sunday morning service fundraiser

Don't let this happen to you
Ask God to protect and direct you
Don't get caught today
In the web of entertainment replacing worship
It does not pay

It only feels good for a day
Entertainment replacing Worship
It's an abomination unto God
It does not pay
Only gets in the way.

Watch and Pray

By Dianne Van der Meer

The Lord will not disappoint you
Blessing your faithfulness today
In spite of
Some leaders around you
Whose lives are dirty
And hidden away
Just watch and pray.

They seem to fear not God
In their dealings
Oh, the games they play,
Don't be a judge
Just watch and pray.

What's done in darkness
Must come to light,
Exposing the dirt,
The Bible says,
Just watch and pray.

The Lord will take the wise
In their own craftiness
That's what the Bible says.
Just watch and pray.

Revelation

By Dianne Van der Meer

A rude awakening
Of the revelation
One, an alcoholic,
One, narcissistic,
One, terminally ill,

Family imperfections
Revealing all at once
Hitting, with a sudden blow
As if wanting me to go

A warrior, I stand
Trusting in the word of God
Is my stance.

Thanks

By Dianne Van der Meer

Thank You, Lord
For this Day
The going is rough,
But I know that you are with me
All the way

As I watch and pray,
Help me this day,
For the going is rough,
But I know that you are with me
All the way.

PART 8:

THE CARIBBEAN

Jamaica

By Dianne Van der Meer

Walking in May Pen Market
For the first time
With my scandal bag*
Swinging in the wind,
A friend watching me, smiling

Why carry
That plastic grocery bag
Looking so funny,
Exposing all yuh groceries
For all ah we, to see

We call it a Scandal bag,
So transparent you see
Exposing all yuh groceries
For all ah we to see

What's so scandalous about my scandal bag?
It works for me
Holding all my groceries
I don't care if you see!

---

* Scandal Bag: Any plastic transparent bag

It's holding my yellow parrot fish
It's holding my doctor fish
It's big enough to hold my blue fish

And it still has room to hold
My tomatoes, sweet potatoes and Cro Cro
What a great market bag
My scandal bag is.

The Wake

By Dianne Van der Meer

Victoria Town in Manchester, Jamaica
Way up past Toll Gate in Clarendon
Two weeks straight
Street party
The culture
It's a Wake
Fit for a king

Neighbors coming
From near and far
Paying last respects
The dead, my friend's Papa

Dies she that brings the community together
Dies he two weeks later
The Rhodens, bringing their community together
Dead sister and now brother

It's party time
Two double weeks in a row
Wake in progress
A big community show

Vendors line the street
Leading to the deceased's house
Selling jerk pork, chicken, fish and souse
Cold beers and Guinness Stout

Breeze blowing, Ganja smelling, strong

Inside the house a live band playing
People dancing
Some praying
A pot of food steaming

Someone shouting

Cook the mannish water
Sure to season it well
Everybody ordering it
To do them well

Natives swear by it
Viagra can't beat it
This mannish water
In the Wake they did order

A brew made from
The brains of a goat
Testicles as well

Mannish Water
They swear, can raise
The dead from hell.

Crooked Cop

By Dianne Van der Meer

Landing on that beautiful Caribbean island
My first visit there
Where the hot springs bubble
And things are dear

A warm welcome in the sizzling sun
Taxi drivers jostling for this one
Rushing each other to carry my suitcase
Arguing who laid eyes on me first, is the case

Now heading to my destination
The driver going over the speed limit
Reggae music blasting
Beat pulsating
Slow down, if you please

To a screeching halt he comes
Traffic Cop flagging him down
Almost hitting the Cop

Cop jumps out of the way
Almost hitting the Cop
Cop gets away

Get out of the car
Before I make you pay
I sure you see me
Flagging you "way down they"
Yuh almost knock me "outta" the way

Scared for the driver
Shaking was I
The cop was ugly
Rough and watching cross eye

No problem man
No sweat
The driver whispering under his breath
Them boys them, corrupt
Everybody know
"Them ah" full of contempt, "yuh" know

Get out the car
The police man shouting
Out of the car
The young man jumping

Shaking was I
Ready to offer words in his defense
Be quiet the next passenger said
With money to pay
That's our defense

Smiling sits the young man
Back in the car
Glancing in his review mirror
The police man standing afar

The young man saying
I am not suppose to tell
He asked me for money
He is corrupt as hell

This money, I must now find
Need to come back
By five o'clock today
Pay him the bribe fine
And my speeding ticket will be just fine.

Trinidad and Tobago

By Dianne Van der Meer

Big Fighting in the Opposition Party
Kamla, surfaced as head of the UNC*
Winning over 13,000 people's votes, so plenty
But still needing more votes from the opposition MPs
To seal a win in the opposition party

Bas, the party lion and founder of the UNC
Surfacing with under 1,500 votes,
From his own party
Citing, robbery

MP** Gopeesingh, the final MP conceding
Giving Kamla the votes needing,
Officially sealing her,
Head of the opposition party
With Bas, screaming
Robbery

Bas, position now, grandfather in sitting
Bas, silently looking
At the baton taken from under him
Power never given

---

*   UNC: United National Congress (A Political Party in Trinidad and Tobago)
**   MP: Member of Parliament

Jack, Chairman of the party
Sides with Kamla and MP Gypsy
To promote the interests of the party,
Jack, a man with a heart for his country

A tough fight election time
Kamla, in a good position
No longer threatened,
Looking to bring party reconciliation

This other MP
A sharp lawyer is he
Now standing alone in the UNC
Seemingly unable to reconcile
With the party's nominee and, his party
Time will tell.

Kamla now head of the UNC
Waving thanks to the people and MPs
With Chutney Soca music blasting
Feeling like Indian arrival day

People dancing, celebrating
Showing the strength of the party
A changing culture
Electing the first woman
As their party leader
Making history

Kamla stands in line for another nominee
As the first woman Prime Minister
Of this little but powerful country
Trinidad and Tobago
She sure was ready
To make history

Joining with four other political parties
Forming the People's Partnership Coalition Party
They did it, a win
Hooray, Kamla
Trinidad and Tobago's first female Prime Minister.

Barbados

By Dianne Van der Meer

Barbados, the homeland of my Grandmother,
Paris and Gibson her Mother and Father
Do you know these names?
I asked a stranger.

Upon hearing her Barbadian accent
That Sounded Familiar
Yes, they are from the same Parish as me
Paris and Gibson from Saint Philip, like me

Their names reveal the Parish, you see.
I could even give you the exact area.
It's East Point in Maverick near me.
Scribbling on a piece of paper, she wrote.

This information for years I sought
Now coming to me
Was it destiny? I thought
Sitting next to her on that bus
This woman from Barbados

Next stop is mine
Pressing the bell
Off the bus she pops
Waving and smiling

Continuing my journey
Wondering what are the odds
Of sitting next to that lady
On a crowded bus

Only time will tell
If her information will help me
To connect with my long lost family
Or maybe this poem will be.

Saint Vincent

By Dianne Van der Meer

"What is ta is, will is."
Concluded a wealthy, unpolished, local
Seated, next to an Ambassador
At a Campaign dinner

Expressing his political views
While reaching for the finger bowl,
Drinking all of its water,
Commenting further
On political matters,
"What is ta is, will is."

Contented with whichever way
The votes went
He concluded the matter
With his thirst quenched.

Grande Riviere

By Dianne Van der Meer

Visit, Grande Riviere
Take deep breaths, inhale fresh air,
Soak, in the best salt water in the western hemisphere,
Perfect for kayaking and surfing
Green and blue waters will entice you there,
That's Grande Riviere.
Where villagers all resemble each other
Like Abraham sperm
A family affair

Located on the northern east tip of Trinidad,
Cough, and it will wake up the neighbor in Venezuela
Spit, and it will land on Tobago shore.
That's Grande Riviere

Gray sandy beaches stretching for miles,
Nesting place, to the Dermochelys Coriacea,
These leatherback turtles bury thousands of eggs
Returning, year after year
That's Grande Riviere

No pollution in the air
Great for watching Meteorites,
A star gazer delight
That's Grande Riviere

Named after the big river of the same name
Flowing from the tip of
Zagaya Mountain, in the Northern Range
Bringing life to a village as the river flows
Soil black like oil
Feeding
Yams, Cassava, Tania and Potatoes
Growing in organic splendor
These edible roots of trees,
Expanding their boundaries,
Going competition with fruit trees
Mangoes, Tonkabean, and Grugrubef
That's Grande Riviere

Coconut trees, short and tall
A harvest ripe for all
Coconut water tasting sweeter than sugar
Sour Lemon making the best lemonade ever
That's Grande Riviere

Vendors selling snake oil, no fake
Extracted from big snake
Snake oil, good for rubbing the waist
Supple waist for sexual escapades
Drink shark oil for the common cold
Steep olive bush in boiling water, a menstrual pain reliever

Catch a moon lit night
A romantic sight
A lover's paradise
That's Grande Riviere

No GPS navigation system needed,
Finding addresses, using light poles as landmarks
Two light poles up, take a left, gone too far
Ask a neighbor to get you there
That's Grande Riviere.

PART 9:

SEASONS

Flora

By Dianne Van der Meer

Hurricane Flora
Do you remember?

I do!

When Flora hit Tobago,
With rain bands, spreading its wings
Across the sky for miles and miles

The sea coming in on Tobago
Overpowering Buccoo
While water from the sky
Caving in roofs
From Charlotteville to Lambeau
And Spaceside, too

Activating Mud slides

A little girl, was I

Learning to pray, when danger lies
Following my grandmother,
Pleading, for mercy from the sky

Our house overlooking the ocean in Trinidad, sits
The sea, looking milky, bitchy, gray and choppy
In a bad mood

Dead chickens floating by,
Our meal for the morning after
Chicken and duck, plucked from the rising waters

Streets, impassable but by boat
Looking like the streets of Venice
In the picture on the wall
Minus the calm and romance
To Venice, I call.

Snow

By Dianne Van der Meer

Look at this Snow
So white and fluffy, declared she,
Spread as far as the eye could see,
Looking like a neat white sheet,
Spread from heaven over the city
It's so pretty!

Winter

By Dianne Van der Meer

So marveled was she
Seeing snow for the first time
This seventy-six-year-old Caribbean Lady

It's raining
She's exclaiming
So marveled was she
Seeing snow for the first time
This seventy-six-year-old Caribbean Lady

The sky is raining down snow like rain
She exclaims
So marveled was she
This seventy-six-year-old Caribbean Lady

Asking a set of questions in a row
Asking, can I eat snow?
Asking, does it turn into water, do you know?
Asking, does it melt away quickly, this snow?
Or vaporizes when the sun shines again?
Where does the city put all this Snow?
Pondering on the snow storm building intensity
So marveled was she
This seventy-six-year-old Caribbean Lady

Come see, put your foot in
So scared was she
Afraid to walk in the snow
She bends to touch the snow
Saying, but how could this be?
So marveled was she
This seventy-six-year-old Caribbean Lady

For the first time
Holding snow in her hand
Watching a sheet of white snow
As far as her eyes could see
I'll rather be perched behind the window
Without gloves and boots
And this heavy winter coat, said she
Watching the heavens rain down snow
So marveled was she
This seventy-six-year-old Caribbean Lady.

Spring

By Dianne Van der Meer

Rising to the fresh of spring
As only evolving from Boston's winter brings

Spring the best season for me,
An escape from the winter blast of Boston

Reading in the Holy Book
Hell is hot
A burning fire
Error or not

Believing hell to be cold,
Confirming is Boston's winter cold

I sometimes wonder
If winter will ever go away
Wanting to escape hell
Like the rich man passing Lazarus, on the way

Longing to see spring,
Heaven at last
Wanting to escape hell
Spring comes at last.

Summer

By Dianne Van der Meer

Now feeling the hot of summer
In Florida
Hot, as ever

They tell me don't complain
It's summer again

Thinking about which season I rather
Spring, summer, autumn or winter
An easy choice for me
Spring!
Best, season ever

Here am I
Stuck in Florida's hot summer
With hurricanes of different names
Lurking all over

Big names
Hugo, Andrew and Katrina

Never knew winds could howl so
Sounding like a clip
From a horror movie

Buckling down to ride out a storm
Forecasters say, only the tailwinds
To suffer my way

Tailwinds I say
Winds howling
Sounding like the sound track from "Jaws" ready to strike
Don't eat me alive

Lights flickering as if bluffing
Now dark

Suddenly remembering
My windows have no shutters
Contemplating running to a nearby shelter
Too late
Darkness dictate
Looking up at the heavens
The clouds bursting with grayish violence
No stars in the heavens

Abruptly aborting its sparking splendor
As if
Shaken by the fierce winds
Interrupting

Royal Palms bending to the ground
In submission
To her majesty
The Wind

Rising again saluting, the wind

South Florida
Shaken out of order
Conceding to this hurricane
In progressive order.

Global Warming

By Dianne Van der Meer

March winds
Feeling like deep winter chills

Raining nonstop for three days
In New England

Winter struggling to transition
Unsettling
Don't want to give up
Confused

Spring's blustery winds
Bringing with it April showers
Putting the weather pattern out of order
A global warming disorder

Ice glaciers melting in Alaska
Tsunami in Indonesia
Big predictions for South America

The earth violently shaking from Haiti to Chile
Leaving its inhabitants empty
Global warming a threat
In the Twenty-first Century.

Autumn

By Dianne Van der Meer

Autumn leaves
So bright and clear
Foliage so beautiful

Mid-October

Leaves in their splendor
Like harvest time for a farmer
Leaves of every size and color

Dropping ripe fruits
Its leaves

A spectacular show of color
Product of a natural act
Untouchable compared to man's creation
That's autumn.

Part 10:

Abuse

Scandal

By Dianne Van der Meer

Scandal in the beautiful city, Boston
Class action suit
Priests running for cover
Not knowing whose name will be called next
Scandal, scandal in Boston

Kids now adults, coming out
Coming out from the closet they shout
I was a little altar boy
When Father tricked me to bow

Bending over, it was all over
Father,
Repeatedly, saying don't tell another

I felt it was my fault
Yet I still told my mother
Repeatedly, Father did it
Saying don't tell another

Mother did not believe
Calling me a liar
She was so fond of Father

Now 30 years later
A confession from Father
He was not the only priest
Running for cover

This scandal rocked Boston
Mother never knew
Now dead

Millions of dollars class action lawsuits
Won
They had to pay
For the many they hurt
Passing their way.

Veins

By Dianne Van der Meer

Standing next to a disabled woman and her lover
Woman, bent over on her walker
Osteoporosis taken over
Sadly looking up from under
At her lover

Man asking, what's wrong with you,
What's the matter?
Woman blurting out
"I want to leave you!"
That's the matter.

Veins on his neck pulsating
Shouting, you cannot leave me! Where will you go?
You cannot leave me! You have no place to go.

Yes! I do, I have three children you know
His eyes charging, as if whipping, while saying
You bitch! Those children don't want you.
You Crazy! You cannot leave me!
Look at you, look at you!
If you leave me, where will you go?

Her drooping eyes telling a story
Helpless, trapped in her body

Looking in, I am wondering,
How many years of Abuse
Has this woman been suffering?

Say No

By Dianne Van der Meer

Abuse, is an oppressive dark place.
It's grip, brass face,
With jaws of an alligator,
Coming to devour,

Teeth laced with poison
Piercing every vein,
Burning like pepper
Blood shedding with every tear
Buckets filling in despair

Long arms wrapping,
Its victims conceding
Feeling like a dead man head lock
Legs dangling

The Abuser requiring silence
In fear, victims keeping the oath
Darkness covers the throat

Look beyond the phantom
Embrace the flicker of light within
Hope of vindication, it brings
Fear keeps the darkness in
Only the power of the mind can dispel

Remember the abuser is an addict
Abusing because he can do it
Needing a fix at your expense
It's time for it to stop

Your life is in your hand
Your strength is in your stand
Say no, to abuse
That's the mindset you must choose
To deliver yourself from your abuser's hands.

She Arose

By Dianne Van der Meer

Up from the ruins
She arose
To tell a story untold
Not just her own
Breaking the silence
She arose

Uncovering ungodliness
From her own
A reflection
Of many on the throne

Men of the cloth
Behaving unseemly
No reverence for God,
Wives, dying in silence
To maintain first lady status

Intimidation, fear, control
Misuse of power
From under that white collar
Feeling no one dear to call for an answer

Clever as ever
So charismatic
Persons outside
Cannot see it

Truth
The story unfolds
Of not love but
Threats, intimidation, fear, control
From under that white collar
In his private abode

Outsiders in denial
Some refusing to know
Deceived by the collar
A veil,
Story not before told

God watching from the back of the veil
First Lady, praying
Hoping to rent the veil

Up from the ruins she arose
Finally realizing
Her story told.

Change

By Dianne Van der Meer

Clutching for life
Holding on to the wind

Clutching for Life
Holding unto straw

A dead end
Only death for her in store

A walking dead
Joy diminish

Run

Only Change
Will Change

The depth of anguish.

Breaking the Silence

By Dianne Van der Meer

Struggling with Cancer
With an abusive spouse
All too common
Yet hidden
No one talks about

Research now leaning
To hearing the voice of female patients, silently screaming
Researchers making the connection, between
Living with cancer and an abusive lover

A double whammy, indeed
Researchers agree
Cancer just does not appear
Stress an entrée
Causing despair

Stress an entrée
Causing despair
Not so rare for cancer to appear

Research now leaning
To learning more
About this leading
But for some too late
Dying in silent abuse
At the hands of their mates

Murder
At the hands of her abusive lover
Her death certificate
Reading Breast Cancer

Ask the children in the house
They know better
Who's the real killer?
It was not cancer

Still hope for others
Who draw strength
Break the silence
Accomplices, die in silence
That's suicidal
When you don't break the silence.

Narcissist Eye

By Dianne Van der Meer

Comparing himself to Job
Job, a biblical man,
Full of Favor,
Favor with God and Man.

Comparing himself to Job
But having no remorse
Pretending to be right,
Through a Narcissist eye

Never feeling wrong
Always admitting he's right
Articulate
Through a Narcissist eye
Not like Job
Job a biblical man
More like Lot,
Another biblical man

An opportunist Lot was
Young, shrewd, full of energy
Riding on Father Abraham's coat
Shadowing like a horsey

Never feeling wrong
Always admitting he's right
Requiring to be admired
Grandiose, his style

Not like Job
Job had empathy
Envious of others
This man was he

Looking yonder like Lot
Looking into the corrupt, greed
Looking back like Lot's wife
Finding himself frozen in time

Feeling entitlement to life
Knowing wrong from right
Manipulation his style
Through a Narcissist eye.

Fresh Mint

By Dianne Van der Meer

She toils during the day,
Perfumes her bed at night,
Her breath as fresh as mint,
Her presence as light

All who saw her
Said, yes that's who she is
Tender, intelligent, lovely
A kind of a wiz[*]

Too bright for him
Too enlightened for him
Loving him

Expecting him to protect her
Instead, becoming her abuser

Locked in pain
Locked in doubt

She hastens to rest without a doubt
He almost sending her spirit to the cloud
God intervened, with a shout.

---

[*] Wiz: Genius

PART 11:

CITY LIFE

Sunrise

Dianne Van der Meer

Sunrise over the concrete jungle
Less impactful
Compared to sunrise overlooking
The Sea of Galilee
Being once there

Any sunrise is a beauty to behold
Marking the dawn of a new day
Today, we have never seen before
Yesterday, we will never see again

Looking like the sun and moon kissing

Like one

Exchanging positions in the morning
Joy of the dawning
Reflection of a new morning.

Tallahassee

By Dianne Van der Meer

Tallahassee sitting in its natural beauty,
With a rich American Indian history
Streets, mascot and communities, with names honoring tribes,
Apalachee, Seminole, Apalachicola and Miccosukee
First tribe, Apalachee; federally not recognized
Seminole, federally recognized
Now Seminole gaming compact, expiring, 2015

Legislators scrambling to consider expanding
Gambling
Holding public hearings
Regarding table gaming
Seminole testifying

Gambling reform nearing
Hoping to avoid compact collapsing
Resulting in court hearing
History in the making.

Wine Research

By Dianne Van der Meer

Walking through Harvard Square
Where all cultures are represented there

Walking through Harvard Square
Where Harvard University's presence
Fills the air

Walking through Harvard Square
Where the homeless gather there, too

Walking through Harvard Square
Where street artists perform
In grand affair

Two drunks came up to me
In Harvard Square

Brown paper bags in hand
Begging for money
They declared

Help our wine research project
We practice it daily right here

Humoring them, wanting to know more
Repeatedly one saying it's for wine research
We conduct it at the liquor store
Then we come out here on the street
Fundraising to do some more
For our wine research
We must go back to the liquor store.

Bus Ride

By: Dianne Van der Meer

Hopping on a bus in the inner-city
Going to the library
Asking the bus driver
Is this bus going past the library?

Route number 23,
Hop on quickly, I'm busy

Tapping my Charlie card
Starting the journey
A crowded bus is not pretty

Motion, motion, bus in motion
An old lady losing her balance
Falling on a teenager
Sitting right in front of her

Swearing coming from this teenager
As the old lady makes eye contact
With this youngster
Laughter bursting
From another teenager
Saying, man she could be
Your mother

In shock the old lady
Regaining composure
Silently watching the teenager
As if to say
I should have been Madea.

Moon Walk

By Dianne Van der Meer

Look, Mama
He is walking funny
Just like you, Mama
Tripping over that
Trash can
He didn't even see.

Shut up, boy
He's just tipsy
You mean like
Moon walking*
Like you, Mama?

Shut up, I said
He is shooting up
What's shooting up, Mama?
Do you shoot up too?
'Cause he's walking just like you

Child, don't test me
Stop talking to me
And eat your candy.

---

* Moon Walking: To lift feet high off the ground while walking, struggling to control foot movement as if to lose balance any minute.

Boo*

By Dianne Van der Meer

Stop requested, stop requested.
Urban living,
A packed bus,
Standing room only,
Each facial expression,
Telling a different story

The rage of a middle-age woman
Relationship gone sour,
Screaming on her cell phone,
Boo, if you want
We could take this
One step further

A mother making conversation
With her teenage daughter
Silence is the answer
From this teenager

Another teenager
Looking vexed with the world,
Robbed of her innocence
Feeding her baby girl

---

* Boo: A slang or vernacular used to identify a boyfriend as in "he's my boo."

A young man sitting beside her
Asking her about his friend
The baby's father
He ain't my boo,
No more.

Fair Shake

By Dianne Van der Meer

Think the innercity
Only has crime and poverty?
Not really
Streets dangerous after dusk
With crime, drugs, police and ambulances
That too
Let this not be your only image of the innercity
There are people just like you and me
With families that care and people that share
Having thanksgiving dinner together every year

A few bad eggs here and there
Neighbors watching out for each other
Children showering under the park sprinklers
Summer days get real hot here
Tall buildings, less trees

Life in the innercity
Some families spanning four generations
That's all they know
Many, with nowhere else to go

Grandma, breezing out on the front porch
Grandpa, hanging out at the barber shop
Shooting the breeze, keeping up on community news

Urban dwellers caring for each other
Finding solace in Church and each other
Parents always looking for opportunities
To bring their families, out of poverty
In the innercity kids want to achieve
Just like in any other community
Kids are taught to say thank you and please

Though the playing field is unequal
The innercity has high achievers
Youth struggling to remain positive
Needing encouragement and incentives
So, next time you sit on the train next to an innercity youth
Don't let the baggy pants and dialect scare you
That's one of our kids
The innercity belongs to me; and, you.

PART 12:

SOCIAL

Milan's Grace

By Dianne Van der Meer

The son of a Milan* was he,
Rising to the occasion of aristocracy,
Displaying fine manners,
Enjoying a new life
Developing exquisite taste
Hidden under was Milan's Grace

Shockingly, refusing to look back
At where he came from and all of that
Wanting never to be reminded of his Milan class,
He marries a woman from the upper class.

Struggling was he
To maintain his new identity,
Trying to fit in outside of his mold,
Always compromising,
His story still untold,
Accepting life as a second class citizen,
Milan, in his new aristocrat role.

---

* Milan: A lower social class person

Folly

By Dianne Van der Meer

A child's folly
Lingering, as an adult
A child's folly
Transferring, into the adult
Never growing up
Damaging, as an adult
Lacking wisdom, having none
Wise in self-importance

A child's folly
Unchangeable when in an adult
Damaging others without a doubt
Leave fools in their folly
The Bible says
Wisdom teaches, just walk away.

King of Pop

By Dianne Van der Meer

King of Pop learning from
King of Soul
We'll miss you, Michael
May God bless your soul

Opening doors of opportunities
Never missing a beat
Dancing that moon walk
No one could ever beat

Sad to see you go
So young, talented, charismatic too
A great show
Sad to see you go

Good business sense
Michael
Why you had to go?
Never saying goodbye
Sad to see you go

Before many could understand you,
Your talents telling the story
Of a super hero to many
Leaving a great legacy

But it was not always easy
You struggled with so much turmoil within,
Dying, never knowing
That the world accepted you
In your own skin.

Rude Awakening

By Dianne Van der Meer

So Brilliant,
Young and strong
Wasting his energy on
Wine, women and song

So beautiful,
Young and strong
Wasting her substance on him

Societal ills
An element of poverty, drugs

Locking its prey in a vacuum
Whose depth only sound
Of a void emptiness
Weightlessness, a sucking in sound

A wake-up call, a shocking reality
Shattering homes
Parents last to know

In denial

Parents

Struggling to make sense
Of sons and daughters they no longer know

Changing lives, changing faces
A new persona
Real impact now unfolding
Yet to be fully discovered

Children left to fend on their own,
Grandparents filling parents' roles,
Welfare and foster care their only support and hope

New births entering
Young parents exiting
Leaving grandparents holding
The next generation now unfolding.

Runaways

By Dianne Van der Meer

For sale, human bodies, trafficking
Common exchange of human cargo
Only fingers pointing
While perpetrators sliding

Victims, our youths
Trapped on the street
Looking for a better life

Some runaways

Caught in drugs, crime and prostitution
Against their will
Telling of a war we must still fight
For our own
Not in Afghanistan, Iraq, Iran or Syria
At home.

DNA Truth

By Dianne Van der Meer

Father, brilliant but absent
Seemingly forgetting his son
Like millions of others do
How often boasting of his son
To the people he knew

Leaving for Africa,
Never experiencing his bundle of joy,
Never seeing him grow up
Never taking him to school
Never tucking him to sleep
Never seeing him achieve

Mother Grieving,
Realizing, this interracial marriage
Not working
The husband leaving,
Back home to Kenya going

In Dad's absence
DNA still working
A brilliant lad just like dad
Dad now sleeping

Mom's style, brilliance and beauty
Penetrating his charm and personality
A fine young man is he
DNA still working
Mom now sleeping

Brought up by grandparents
Such stability making a difference
DNA still working
Even after mom and dad sleeping

When the offspring
Of the roots of Kenya
Returning to roots, now as the President of
The United States of America
All Kenya stops to salute
Their hero, in honor of DNA Truth.

Hubris

By Dianne Van der Meer

Hubris* unfolding
Tragedy waiting
Two Lovers

Seeing but not seeing
Blinded by love overpowering
Romantically celebrating
But Hubris unfolding

Blinded by pride overpowering

Each person slowly dying
Hubris Escalating

Lovers not hearing
Lovers not seeing
Hubris wheeling and dealing
Killing the love from the beginning

Now Hubris fully taking over
Relationship going under
Hubris wheeling and dealing
Inevitable death by hubris seeming.

---

* Hubris: Arrogance or Excessive pride: usually referring to humans trying to act like Greek gods

Pack Fever

By Dianne Van der Meer

The alleged game
Teenage pregnancy pack the fame
Originated from a high school in Massachusetts
Teenage group pregnancy the intent

See those Bellies protruding at the onset
A product of broken homes
A product of social disorder
A product of moral breakdowns
A lack of attention

Pack Fever
Teenage pregnancy pack fame
Comparing growing tummies the game

Pack Fever
Teenage boys and girls
Promiscuously and willingly participating
Under peer pressure some yielding

Pack Fever
After-school showdowns like gladiators
Teenage girls, teenage boys settling scores
Laying claim to baby's father
Laying claim to baby's mama
Pointing fingers at each other

Pack Fever
By the lockers they congregate
Announcing baby's arrival date
Over cell phones pictures circulate
Of new born babies and proud mummies

Sealing the pregnancy pack with secrecy
Anticipating whose next
Texting the juicy gossip
Who's sexing who
Whose baby due
Class in session
Pack Fever

Teenage boys striding through the hallways
Chest protruding
Boastfully laughing
Comparing notes
Some denying fathering

Catastrophe pack fever causing
Dangerous thought, pack fever export
Shame on school administrators
For allegedly ignoring pack fever
For allegedly ignoring parents' calls

No adults taking blame
Pointing fingers at each other, their game
Quickly sealing lips on the matter
Pack Fever a product of
Post twentieth century social blunder.

War

By Dianne Van der Meer

War in the east
War in the west
War in the homes
No one can rest

War in the north
War in the south
War on the streets
No one can shout

Civil War
Ethnic War
Money War
All kinds of Wars

Afghanistan celebrated nine years of war
Marking the day with eight fallen American soldiers
America mourns,
Rivers run red

Fighting continues
Iran war adding to the issues
Syria's chemical weapon used
Raining down on its own
A global threat
The blood of war and rumors of wars.

Mother's Cry

By Dianne Van der Meer

Young men, young women on the streets
Listen to a mother's cry
That child no longer she knows
That child no longer knows her

Needing to be rescued from self
Overcome by drugs, sex and deception
Lacking wisdom, strength, discipline

Intervention

A mother's cry, painful and real
Helplessly looking at her dying breed
Knowing if help does not come soon
The options are real
Jail, death, rehab, the deal

A mother's cry, painful and real
Helplessly looking at her dying breed
Never giving up
Looking beyond the despair
To hope and prayer.

Legacy

By Dianne Van der Meer

In pursuit of legacy
That outlives us all
Good contributions of mankind
It will live on

It's good to know
When long gone
Legacy lives on.

Addictive Society

By Dianne Van der Meer

An over drugged society
Cannot produce a healthy next century

An over indulgence in food society
Cannot produce a healthy next century

An obese society
Cannot produce a healthy next century

An affinity to addictions in society
Cannot produce a healthy next century

We are lost without a plan
A plan to change
Social habits
Turning to education and intervention
As early as birth
A viable option.

Street Drug Methadone

By Dianne Van der Meer

Meth on the streets, a preferred drug of use
Meth users rejoicing, no longer visiting their drug-dealers
State government their new supplier
Drug dealers losing big business
Free supplies available at the city's Meth clinics
Register and stop by the met lab as early as 4:00 A.M.
Guaranteeing an early fix, reaching to work on time,
Some for their hospital shifts.

State government the new supplier
Who would expect a street drug distribution with tax payers'
dollars?
How can we explain this to our sons and daughters?
What would I say to my grandson when he grows up?

Who's using these Meth labs?
You might be shocked.

Not just
Farm workers,
The unemployed brother
Or that homeless man in the shelter
But blue and white collar workers, regular consumers

Pulling up at Meth Labs
In the twilight
Satisfying a drug habit
Getting free, legal street drugs
State government the new supplier

Just up the street
Another similar facility
Distributing clean needles to the needy.

An Addict

By Dianne Van der Meer

Listening to this man
An addict

Sharing about the 12-Step program helping him
A principle based on accepting a higher being
Saint Jude he ascribes as his being

Now recognizing his calling
Once an addict, always an addict admitting,
Dependency on drugs and alcohol once his high,
Twelve-step program, a new high

Relapsing

Describing need for change
An Alcohol Anonymous group saying
He's the man on the stool,
Always talking of the future,
Sitting on that very stool,
Twelve years later

Going nowhere
Still on that stool
Talking of the future
Sitting on that very stool
Twelve years later

A wake up call
Everything lost
Hits rock bottom
Surrendering to the cause

Remembering,

Another Alcoholic Anonymous, saying
"If nothing changes, nothing changes."

An Enabler

By Dianne Van der Meer

Myself an enabler
I could not see
Love camouflages
The denial in me

Maternal instinct steps in
Still blinded
Then I see

To wake up
And not enable
Is a startling reality.

PART 13:

REMEMBERING
SENATOR KENNEDY

Next Passage

By Dianne Van der Meer

Massachusetts' Senator, Edward Moore "Ted" Kennedy
Writes to Pope Benedict
Anticipating his next passage
Needing forgiveness
Asking the Holy Father for prayers
Making peace with his God
Before he disappears

Re-committing to the Catholic faith
Expressing his mother's faithfulness to the faith
Kennedy confesses his imperfectabilities
Wanting to right his wrongs
Making his path clear
Needing the Holy Father's prayer

The letter, recounting his fight
As champion of the poor
Like Mother Theresa

The letter, recounting
His fighting to end the war
Acknowledging his education and
Healthcare voting records, the law
To benefit the poor,
Opening doors of economic opportunities for all
Senator Kennedy writes to the successor of Pope John Paul,
the second

A confession on reflection
Timely
Requesting the Holy Father's support
Holy Father responded, forgiveness
Senator Kennedy, now passed on, sleeping
Pope Benedict abruptly retiring.

Funeral Procession

By Dianne Van der Meer

Funeral Procession
Fit for a king
Slowing passing by
On a rainy Saturday morning
In August

The world watches
The hearse slowly passing by
That wet morning
The streets lined with passersby
Waving goodbye

Funeral Procession
Fit for a king
The first Royal family of Massachusetts
In mourning

A legend passing on
The senior senator, was he
Called the Lion of the Senate
Pushing a liberal ideology
King of the jungle,
Gaining respect from
The left and right

A legend passing on
This senior member
Of the Royal Family
Ted Kennedy, was he
Lion, husband, father
Uncle, friend and buddy
Ted Kennedy

A legend passing on
Big was his heart and energy
Fighting a good fight
Losing to brain tumor
Losing but still winning
Leaving a legacy
Ted Kennedy.

PART 14:

POLITICAL

Gaddafi Ramajay*

By Dianne Van der Meer

United Nations General Assembly
Sixty-fourth meeting in session
Colonel Muammar Gaddafi of Libya appears
Present, Gaddafi, first time in 40 years
Entering with theatrical fanfare
Colonel Gaddafi appears

Gaddafi, a man known to many as
Muammar al-Khaddafi
Whose name has over sixty ways of spelling
One could be used for each general assembly meeting

Gaddafi, present after 40 years
America's international unwillingness
To go it alone, all the way
Making way for Gaddafi to come this way

Gaddafi seizes his moment in history
Rumbling on for ninety-eight minutes
Addressing the United Nations Assembly
Dramatically reading from his hand-written notes
In boyish folly

---

* Ramajay: Showing off

Tossing the United Nation's Assembly Constitution behind
him
As if truly believing his presence at the Assembly
Is America's pardon, to him

Treating others as foe
Embracing Venezuela, Iran and China
Gaddafi feeling empowered
Calling America's 46th.President his son
Ramajaying as if imparting wisdom

Speech
Embarrassing as a head of a nation
Gaddafi, scanning the audience
A kodak moment to remember
One delegate rubbing his eyes fighting to keep awake
Two others laughing
Gaddafi still Ramajaying
Other representatives respectfully sitting
Quietly listening, their facial expression
Showing their disgust at Gaddafi Ramajaying.

Scotland Yard

By Dianne Van der Meer

Set free by Scotland Yard Authority
To die in peace and dignity
After being found guilty
Of bombing Pan Am Flight 103,
Flying over Lockerbie

Doctors gave him time to live
Three months more
Before prostate cancer
To which he must submit

Mercy extended frees him to live
His life with friends and family
Mercy afforded him

Where is the mercy
To which he gave
None to Pan Am Flight 103
The Passengers all killed

Hard to forgive
A man who's showing no remorse
For the lives he killed
No remorse at all

For the families left behind
They will never see
Their loved ones again
No goodbyes afforded them

Returning home to a hero's welcome
Making a mockery of the system
Pardon by Scotland Yard this day
A slap in America's face that day

Some blamed Britain
For cutting a deal
Influencing Scotland Yard
The mercy freedom to reveal

Britain's Prime Minister
Swearing to reporters
No deal, no deal, none whatsoever
Reiterating it was solely a Scotland Yard decision
One England had no jurisdiction over, whatsoever

Telling Reporters, President Obama
Did not shun him
At the United Nations meeting
Over this Scotland Yard freeing

Telling Reporters
Britain is America's ally forever
Still the families of bombing victims
Awaiting an answer
Wondering why was there no consideration
Afforded them in this Scotland Yard matter?

Flight 103

By Dianne Van der Meer

A long time this be 1988
But still a fresh memory
Pan Am Flight 103

Caught at the hands of
A Libyan Secret Agent
Over Lockerbie

What a tragedy this be
Pan Am Flight 103
Gone over Lockerbie
At the Hands of al-Megrahi

Two hundred and seventy dead
Mostly Americans
Leaving a bitter memory
At the hands of al-Megrahi

What a disgrace this now create
To see Scotland Yard set
Al-Megrahi free
On humanitarian grounds
To return to his country

Dying slowly of prostate cancer
In his own country,
In peace
Among Friends and family

Where is the justice
For the dead over Lockerbie
Where is the justice for the
Families' memories
None.

Salute President Obama

By Dianne Van der Meer

News sending shockwaves through the air
Dancing breaks out in Times Square
Celebrations everywhere

First, African American, First Lady of the United States of
American
Waving to the crowd
Representing change
First, African American, President of the United States
The First family

A campaign well run
Talking change
Seeing one nation instead of polarization
Appealing to the younger generation

A tight race, well ran
Bowling out Senator Hillary Clinton
Surfacing as the democratic nominee
Hitting a double whammy
Facing Hillary and husband Bill Clinton, the beloved
two-term President of the United States of America,
Obama, a rookie

Securing the democratic nominee
Now set to run for president of this super country
Against Republican John McCain
A respected veteran
With an unknown running mate Sarah Palin
Shooting to stardom

Campaign fundraising getting ridiculously out of hand
Candidates comparing their financial hand
New, internet fundraising scoring high
Exciting first time voters
In true democratic style

Internet fundraising, a political strategy
Of Post Twentieth Century.

PART 15:

HEALTH CARE

Placebo*

By Dianne Van der Meer

Positive thoughts get you everywhere
Negative thoughts destroy you, I swear
The mind, such a powerful tool

Can build you up
Can break you down
It's how you think
Not how you sound

The mind a gallery space
Can create a placebo
A pleasing thought, awaits

The mind, a rigid place
Can create a Nocebo**
Flipping like a pancake

The mind such a powerful tool
Dictating winning or losing
You deciding
Thinking Nocebo, harming self
Thinking Placebo, healing self.

---

*   Placebo: I will please
**   Nocebo: I will harm

Emergency Unit

By Dianne Van der Meer

A visit to the ER Unit
Crying out for chest pains
Feeling like a cardiac arrest
About to take place

The complexity of the ER staff
You just won't believe it
Chest pains being investigated
Just like a crime scene unit
Resident doctors shifting in and out
All asking the same questions without a doubt
How severe is the pain?
Tell me on a scale of one to ten.

This one resident doctor asking,
Does the chest pain hurt when you are sleeping?
No kidding
In my sleep
I just couldn't tell
On a scale of one to ten.

Health Care Reform

By Dianne Van der Meer

It's the Twenty-first Century
Medical science advancing
Health care woes increasing
Democrats and Republicans arguing
Over Health Care Reform
While pharmaceutical
Companies profiting

Drug prices gone through the sky
CEOs living high
Lobbyist salaries high, high

HMOs over-charging
Leaving us to die
If we cannot pay
I wonder why

Canada has Universal Health Care
With cheaper drug prices everywhere
For the same drugs selling here

USA Pharmaceutical Companies
Acting like they don't care
Doctors protecting themselves
HMOs not supporting the changes in Health Care

Health Care Reform
That's all we hear
Debating in committee
That's all we hear

Olympia Snowe, Senator for Maine,
Was the first Republican
To support President Obama's
Proposed healthcare legislation
The Affordable Health Care Act
Nicknamed, Obama Care
Snowe having to defend her position

The Health Care Bill,
Getting this far
Franklin Delano Roosevelt
America's 32nd. President
Would declare with cheers, hooray!

For his attempts
To reform health care
Almost 100 years earlier
Did not go far

Lacking support and care
But now it's here
Universal Health Care
Discussions in the Public Square
Government shutdown October 2013.

Biologics

By Dianne Van der Meer

Small biotech companies struggling,
Big biotech companies flourishing
Venture capitalists investing
In hope of reaping
From a market that's continually seeking

Life science growing
Biotech companies seeking
Seeking biologics* instead of generics
Seeking biologics as, alternatives

Big shifts happening in drug manufacturing
Chemically based pharmaceuticals matter
Giving way to Biologics derived from live matter
Securing a future for live science that matters

Biologics costing high
Sky rocketing through the blue sky
Pharmaceutical companies still riding high
Pharmaceutical lobbyists' salaries outrageously high

---

* Biologics: A preparation, such as a drug, a vaccine, or an antitoxin, that is synthesized from livings organisms

Lobbyists' influence big in congress
Pushing Biologics to floor vote
When not even the Committee Chairman, could tell

Chairman lobbying his colleagues from the floor
Pharmaceutical Lobbyist sealing it long before
Angered and shocked
Committee Chairman not knowing before
Who will vote against or for

Pharmaceutical lobbyists taking
The power from the Chair
Watching Roll Call* from the gallery
Watching Chairman on the floor
Shouting in despair
Only time will tell how biologics will fare.

---

*   Roll Call: List, register or recording system

Trauma

By Dianne Van der Meer

Trauma like acid
Cutting away dross,
Opening old wounds,
Ripping through
A solid foundation,
Taking with it,
Building blocks.

Discovering Wells
You could never tell
From deep inside
Hidden Mines

The treasure of the quarry
After the excavation
Is the strength to seek

Trauma blasting the Well
Shattering it well
Exposing it in plain sight
Not even dynamite could work this site
Trauma exposing the foundation of your very life

Finding the voice
That only trauma can bring
Do not ignore it
Just dig right in

Trauma can be negative
Trauma can draw out positive
Which one you choose
Determines how you deal with it

Don't let trauma kill you
Though it will surely faze you
Dig deep into the Well
And allow it to heal you as well.

PART 16:

VINDICATION

Reflection

By Dianne Van der Meer

Looking at myself in the mirror
New lines
Stretching across my forehead

Looking as prominent
As blue lines
Stretching across white paper

Looking at myself in the mirror
I see
A deep horizontal crease
Running through my third eye
Stopping at my hair line

Set like the blue margins
On a ledger book

When did it appear?
Seem so sudden
In prominence it glares
Telling my story and more
Signs of battle and war
With a drop jaw of pain and grief

Counting tiny lines under my eyes
Its contour cracking and dry
Like the cracks in the Sahara desert, so dry

Looking into the mirror
My reflection steering back at me
From beyond the grief
New life I see.

Trapped

By Dianne Van der Meer

Trapped in a vacuum
That sucked me in
I don't know why
But I got sucked in

I tried to get out
It kept sucking me in
I don't know why
But I got sucked in

Tumbling to the sound of
This vacuum sucking me in
A free fall drop
Experiencing within

Then, a sudden stop
As quickly as I fell in
Like a rocket blast
The vacuum
Expelling me from within.

Vindication

By Dianne Van der Meer

Two wives, of the same name
One husband, theirs,
Known for fame
Meticulously manipulating
Shadowed in his fame
Wife, number one
Wife, number two
Two wives, of the same name

In the beaming, bright, sizzling summer
One August day to remember
Hands clasps, oh, so somber
In criminal court,
A day to remember

The same August day to remember
Two years before, when he buried the other
In the cemetery,

The two bear the same name as he remembers
And they had that same August day to remember
When the end came for the other
After 40 years of somber

Then, like a flash of déjà vu[*]
August comes again to remember
Number two, being put to slaughter
After just two years of somber
At the hands of her abuser

Acquittal! In arrogance, expected the abuser
But only God could vindicate her
From the hands of this deceiver

A repeat of the burial of the same name other
Oh no! To God, cried her mother,
He cannot bury my daughter, mother praying
Case called

With quick verdict on the abuser
Guilty, Guilty, the jury sounded to each other
Vindicating, the same name other.

---

[*] Déjà vu: A feeling of experiencing something for the first time that you feel
you have experienced before

REFERENCES

Access Genealogy. *Massachusetts Indian Tribes.* Retrieved, October 16, 2009, from www.accessgenealogy.com/native/massachusetts/

Brooks-Motl, H. *Aristocracies of One:* On British and American Poetry. As posted on Contemporary Poetry Review. Retrieved, April 27, 2010, from http://www.cprw.com/Misc/usbrits.htm

CNN Politics. *Excerpts from Kennedy's letter to Pope Benedict XVI.* Retrieved, October 15, 2009, from http://www.cnn.com/2009/POLITICS/08/29/kennedy.pope.letter/

Crane, H. (2006). *Complete poems and selected letters.* New York: Library of America.

Discover Trinidad and Tobago: the definitive guide to the islands. Retrieved, May 6, 2009, from http://www.discovertnt.com

Emanuel, J. A., & Gross, T. L. (1968). *Dark symphony: Negro literature in America:* New York, NY: Free Press, a division of MacMillan Publishing Co.

Frost, R. (1993). *The road not taken and other poems.* Mineola, NY: Dover Publications.

Gates Jr., H. L., & McKay, N.Y. (Eds.), (1996). *The Norton anthology of African American literature.* New York, NY: WW Norton & Company.

Hartman, H. (2007). *Groundhog day: The adventures of Punxsutawney Phil, Wiarton Willie, and Pothole Pete.* Retrieved on February 5, 2010, from http://www.infoplease.com/spot/groundhogday1.html

Hass, R. (1998). *Poet's choice: Poems for everyday life.* New York, NY: HarperCollins Publishers

Lowell, R. (2007). *Life studies and for the union dead.* New York, NY: Farrar, Straus and Giroux

Redmon-Fauset, J. (1999). *Plum bum*: Boston, MA: Beacon Press.

Roses, L. E., & Randolph, R. E. (1997). *Harlem renaissance and beyond: biographies of 100 black women writers.* Cambridge, MA: Harvard University Press

Texas A&M AgriLife Extension. *Mosquito.* Retrieved, May 6, 2009, from http://insects.tamu.edu/fieldguide/bimg220.html

Watts, D. *Trinidad and Tobago.* Retrieved, May 6, 2009, from http://www.britannica.com/EBchecked/topic/605453/Trinidad-and-Tobago

Whitman, R. (1982). *Becoming a poet: source, process and practice.* Waukesha, WI: Kalmbach Publishing Company, Books Division

ABOUT THE AUTHOR

Motivational speaker, pastor and author, Dianne Van der Meer was born on the island of Trinidad in the West Indies. She is the founder of Christians Supporting Community and Living Water Christian Fellowship. Her first book, ***Out on a Limb with No place to Hide, Exposing Defeat While Rising to Victory***, is an inspirational autobiography. Ms. Van der Meer is a doctoral candidate in Higher Education, Leadership. She holds a post graduate degree, the Certificate of Advanced Graduate Studies in Administration, Planning and Policy from Boston University and a Master of Education Degree from Cambridge College.

Ms. Van der Meer has worked in Massachusetts in various departments of state government. She served as a research analyst in the Massachusetts House of Representatives, assistant to the Vice Chancellor for Academic Affairs, Policy and Planning at the Board of Regents of Higher Education, and, taught, in an adjunct capacity, in both private and public institutions of higher education in Massachusetts.

Ms. Van der Meer embraces mentoring and volunteerism and has served as a trustee on numerous boards, including the

Benjamin Banneker Charter School; Cambridge Substance Abuse Task Force, Cambridge, Massachusetts; Seminary of the East in Dresher, Pennsylvania; and the YWCA, Cambridge, Massachusetts. She was a visiting Chaplain at the Boca Raton Community Hospital and a trained volunteer member of Boca Raton Community Emergency Response Team, (CERT). She served as a voting member on West Boca Medical Center, Investigative Review Board (IRB) in Boca Raton, Florida.

Ms. Van der Meer is the petitioner of a proposed Consumer Protection legislative Senate Bill No. 412 filed in the Commonwealth of Massachusetts – An Act Relative to Homeowners' Insurance Coverage and Toxic Drywall.

A mother of three, an avid traveler, and art collector, she currently resides in Florida where she is an Educational Policy Analyst at the Florida Department of Education.

The author, Dianne Van der Meer,
welcomes your comments
vandermeer.dianne@gmail.com